EPIC RITES PRESS

frostbitten

---

poetry by Mark Walton

First edition. Printed in Canada.

Editor: Wolfgang Carstens
Interior: Wolfgang Carstens
Illustrations: Elizabeth A. Soroka
Photograph by Jonathan Dredge
Banner by Ego Rodriguez
Exterior: Pablo Vision

ISBN 978-1-926860-00-8

For more information about *Frostbitten* (and other books and publications from Epic Rites Press) please address: Epic Rites Press, 240 - 222 Baseline Road, Suite #206, Sherwood Park, Alberta, T8H 1S8 and/or contact Wolfgang Carstens at epicritespress@gmail.com.

Epic Rites Press: "because all our fingers are middle ones" ™

To Keith – for being there all the time

author's note

I owe a debt of gratitude to Joe Santini and James O'Riordan for getting me started, to Andi Langford Woods for encouraging me to step out of the comfort of Bristol's Acoustic Night and into the world, and to Chris Madoch for giving me the confidence to call myself a Poet.

I'd like to thank all the poetry and spoken word promoters who create the spaces for people to perform and be heard, and to the community of poets who have provided encouragement, fellowship and support.

In particular I'd like to thank Uli Lenart and Jim MacSweeney at "Gay's The Word" and Jonny Dredge and Ego Rodriguez for their assistance in promoting the initial chapbook.

Frostbitten would never have come to pass without Wolfgang Carstens and Epic Rites Press and I'm honoured to be in the company of all those who work in blood.

Finally a special "thank you" to E. Amato for her friendship, support, advice and invaluable assistance in editing this volume.

– Mark Walton

Contents

FROSTBITTEN

WHAT THE HEART NEEDS TO HEAL

FROSTBITTEN

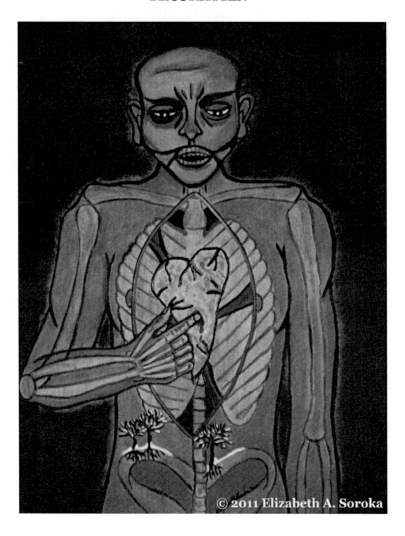

Results

I was supposed to meet you there.
Joint appointments,
news shared.

But arriving early
through the late afternoon
traffic noise,
I give my name,
take a number,
and find a place
amongst the assorted
shamefaced, nervous,
cocky, boys.

Doors swing open
and a white coat breezes through.

"Number 152, follow me.
The Doctor will see you…"

"Now? But… hold on
I was waiting…"

And suspended a moment
between disappearing coat tails
and tugging heartstrings,
I look back,
through the unlit waiting room
to the sunlit street.

No familiar silhouette appears
to hold me here,
so I'm dragged along

in the slipstream
of unaccustomed
clinical efficiency.

Doors close and I take a seat.

A grave look.
A chill descends.

"It's bad news I'm afraid."

Something deep inside me tears.
Something ends.

My disembodied voice
answers questions
as my phone vibrates
against my thigh,
and I imagine you waiting.

Anxious.
Abandoned.
Unknowing.
I tell the doctors
of your expected arrival
and they leave
to speak to you,
giving me no indication
of your news.

My turn to wait,
anxious and alone.

Separated by grey
partition walls.

Numb to the bone.

Minutes congeal
like bad blood.

I'm recalled from my daze
by the phone's vibrate.
Your message,
angry, scared.

The tear widens,
and the broken rubble
that was my heart
crumbles some more.

There's a knock at the door.

The handle turns
and you're there.

A living ghost.

Our eyes meet
and I'm lost in blue,

"It's bad news Baby."
"I know. Me too."

And we reach across
the broken silence,
to hold pale imperfect flesh.

Offering ineffective apologies
for all the stupid, stupid, mistakes

The Maze

My memories of meeting you
are kind of scattered.
My mind shattered by pills.
Glittering fragments
splintered on the dance floor,
picking up reflections
from the mirror-ball lights
and the whites of eyes.

I'm feeling alright.

It's dark and hot
and I'm lost in the rhythm,
submerged as the bass quickens through me.

Someone pushes past
and I surface in a panic,
gulping air and looking 'round,
and you're there beside me.

Smooth, tight, white body.
Jaw set, eyes wide.
A handsome young lad
as lost as I am.

You turn,
and with a smile
you break the frozen drug mask
into pieces.
And beneath it,
dark eyes dance.

Damn, you're handsome.

And I want some.

But before I can say a word,
the warmth of your smile
hits my chest,
breaks in a wave over my head,
and in a rush,
I'm submerged once more.
Before I disappear completely,
you grab my hand
and whisper in my ear,

"Follow me."

You lead me through the
labyrinth of passages
and stairs,
through a sea of sweating flesh
and beer and piss,
to God-knows-where.
Somewhere cooler, calmer,
with people seated everywhere.

A low buzz instead of a tom-tom beat.

You say:
"Come here,
Chill out,
Sit there."

I slide down the wall
to the floor,
legs apart.

You sit between them,
cool back to my chest.
My arms around you
cross your heart,
my chin upon your shoulder.
We're a perfect fit,
though I'm guessing
I'm a few years older.

"So, what's your name..?"
Well it's a start.

"What've you done?"
"Where are you from?"
"Want some water? gum? anything?"
"What?-thing? Can I…? What?"
(sigh)
"Doesn't matter… Kiss me."
A low hum and people stare
at the two skinhead boys over there.
Girls smile. Boys glare.

"What d'you do?"
"What you into?"
"Anything really, what about you?"
"Take me home and find out."

More disjointed,
drug-fucked, dirty talk,
'til the words run out,
and pills kick in again,
and the filthy beat
coming through the floor,
drags us down, down, down,
once more into the music.

The Allotment

I sit,
watching you
stood there,
stretching backwards
into the hill.
Tracing the arc
of your body
with my
eyes.

Downslope,
birdscarers
(plastic bags
on bamboo sticks),
crackle archly
in the wind.
White and
noisy as gulls.

Above you
a rainbow curves,
vibrant
against the
battleship clouds
gathering in
a far away,
sea blue,
sky.

And in the gulf between,

I sit.

And as you stretch,
I trace the arc
of your body,
of the birdscarers,
of the rainbow,
of the hill itself.
Absently noting
the points of intersection,
and anticipating war.

Nine Wishes

I wish I'd never looked now.
Never taken the careless opportunity
to see who the message came from,
or what it said.

My need to know
over-riding your right to privacy.

I wish I'd never seen the words
that told me what you'd done,
behind my back
and how much fun you'd had.

Too much information
for my overactive imagination.

I wish you hadn't lied to me,
or blinked at me in
slowly dawning comprehension,
as you realised
that you'd been caught out in your deception.

I wish you hadn't gone ahead
and made the meeting prearranged.
Leaving me alone to my devices,
whilst you indulged your pleasures
and your secret, unshared vices.

I wish that things were different,
that the trust remained untarnished.
That each phone call,
and each absence,
didn't fill me with such anguish.

I wish for naive innocence returned.
I wish the fresh green leaves of love
remained unburned.

I wish I'd had more self respect
and that I'd simply walked away
and never told you what I'd seen.

I wish that it was you, not me,
left stood bewildered and bereft,
and wishing for what might have been.

For A Friend

Boyfriend-dodging for stolen kisses
in recessed darkness.
You, rubber clad, mohawked,
dangerous looking.
A friendship seeded in furtive
suckfuckfumbled moments.

We swap numbers.

Waking next morning I find your cock strap
in the pocket of my jeans,
warmsoft leather between my fingers,
and, playing Prince Charming,
I come to your house to return it.

You look smaller in daylight.
Glasses on.
Mohican softtousledblond.
Both more sheepish
than last night's fuckclub bravado.

Pushed against the wall for more slowgrope kisses,
"Can't stay, Sexy – I'll be back tho."

But then you're gone.

Back to the metropolis.
Convalesced and West Countried out.
Bored and horny for more.

Business trips brought new adventures.
Cheap King's Cross hotel rendezvous.

Running like wolves through neon Soho,
leering and mischief making.
Friendship forged in
Stella and ketamine.

Mornings waking bruised and confused.

But we survive confusion and contusions,
diagnoses and suicide bombers,
breakdowns and overdoses.
We share confidences and condolences,
and when the bullshit mask of confidence slips,
there's no questions,
just the softest of soft shoulders,
or the sharpest of whiplash quips.

Each the other's "other boyfriend."
The one who knows,
who sees, sideways maybe,
through the jokes and the jackass laughs,
the go-on-then-just-another nights.

Brotherlover,
who knows where the bodies are buried,
where the self-destruct button lies,
and just how close the finger hovers over it.

And with each hard truth
the respect grows,
the bond strengthens,
and catching the glint in your eye
we down another,
light a defiant cigarette,
and laughing, "Dare you," disappear
into another suckfuckfumbled Soho night.

It's A Queer Thing

It's a queer thing.

That fleeting spark of recognition
may lead to ignition on many levels,
so I wonder if we are genetically programmed
or culturally conditioned to be so reductive?
The mission all too frequently to bed.
The head-long rush to sex
before exploring other connections
that we crave to keep our minds and spirits fed.

But fortune favours the brave
and so we rush to conquer,
when perhaps a wiser man would stop
to ponder the consequences
of so many raised hopes
and dropped defences.

Serially compromised and undermined
to the point of total collapse,
or shored up by chemicals
self medicated or prescribed.
Disinhibited by a cocktail of alcohol, proteases,
anti-depressants and impotence remedies.

"I can see from the look on your face
that you're medicated ridged mate."

Take my friend for instance
– you can have him by the hour –
and over a glass of fine wine,
for which his choice of career
has allowed him to develop a taste,

he confides that the secret of his success
is not the fleeting rush of sex,
but the pleasure of his company.
Like whores down the ages he knows
that half the time his punters
are paying for the conversation.
Some kind, any kind, of connection.

I refrain from asking to what extent
it's the kindness of strangers,
as much as the wages,
that keep him playing the game.

Imagine then the scene if we could
see each other's needs for what they are.
If on walking into a bar instead of seeing only
abs, pecs and ready sex,
we could ascertain the hopes and fears,
the love and pain, the latent creativity
just below the carefully honed surfaces,
and perhaps proffer our own offerings in return.

Instead we make do with our constrained liberation.
Our unrequited aggression always unconsummated.
The creativity in our bones stifled and subjugated
into a shuffling parade of passive transgression.

So next time you see that guy
with the lean and hungry look in his eye
just think for a minute.

Perhaps what he really needs...
is a damn good talking to.

Cerne Abbas

I'm striding up a grassy slope,
bracing my body against its steepness.

Above me, over its brow,
a mid-day half-moon rises.
Faded goddess of fertility.

To my left, over the curve of its flank,
a priapic stone-cut giant hides,
hemmed in by chicken wire.
Gulliver in Lilliput.

A family scramble up the hill behind me,
"Daddy, Daddy, what's behind the fence?"

The father turns, "Just a sign, Sweetheart,"
and, catching my smile, he returns it.
Embarrassed at his embarrassment.
Seeking collusion in the protection of innocence.

At the top, the north wind
robs the spring sunshine of its warmth,
and I sit, meditating on the meaning
of the chalk-soft cock,
rock hard for unknown hundreds,
maybe thousands, of years.

Its dubious provenance seems
a fitting symbol of its
masculine sexuality.
A big stone bastard,
obvious but unacknowledged.

The family,
mother, father, daughter, dog,
straggle up the incline towards me and I breathe deeper.

To my chest. To my core. To my groin.

And from somewhere deep inside,
sadness rises.
The possibility of fatherhood twice undone
by the infectious conspiracy
of preference and pathology.

Another windblown future tumbles by.

Childhood laughter brings me back
to Dorset downland,
struggling to spring to new life
in the persistent chill
of this protracted winter.

A lone butterfly dances back and forth through the fence,
and birds, confidently nesting in topmost braches,
promise a fair summer.

I pick up a shard of chalk, keepsake white fragment,
and, rising to my feet, survey the village sheltered below.

Ordered. Settled. Domestic.

Breathing deep once more,
I take comfort in the wind whipped vigour of the hillside,
its hardness jolting through me
as I stride back down the steep, stubbled slope.

Chalk-stone slowly eroding to powder in my pocket.

New Routine

I have a new routine.

Once a week
I take the empty pill box,
and I sit cross legged on the quilt,
covered in bottles and blister packs,
that crack and rattle
like an overactive child's activity mat.

Surrounded by the primary coloured capsules,
and the Monday-Tuesday-Wednesday lids,
my weekly task is to count the daily doses
into their compartments
where they'll stay safely hid.
It's a never ending nursery game
played out on the bed.

One-two-three-four,
check there's no one outside the door,
when the game stops…,
… you're dead.

I have a new habit,
or at least I'm trying to acquire one.
It's funny
how the old ones
you want to kick,
just stick.
Whilst the new ones,
the necessary ones,
the ones that trade compliance
for consequences,
are so damn hard.

Requiring an
electronic beep
each evening,
just to remind me to eat,
and to slide back
the labelled cover,
to reveal today's dose
of candy-colour.

Then it's;
one for Acyclovir,
two for Ritonovir,
three for Atazanovir,
four for Truvada.

Some days are easy.
Some are harder.

But I've got a new trick.
It's all in the wrist.

I can sneak them from my pocket
whilst you look the other way,
and quickly knock them back
as you catch the waiter's eye
to ask if we can pay.
You didn't see a thing
although you've noticed a new glow,
and tell me I look good,
you think that I should know.
I'd tell you that it's jaundice
but don't think that I should.

Side effects can ruin the flow...
... of conversation.

You see I have a new pulse.

It's not in my wrist
and not in my throat.
It's an ache, a throb,
a pain in the neck.

The traitorous glands
that gave virus shelter,
that swelled and ached
until those chemicals took over,
no longer hard under probing fingers
(the Braille signifiers of disease).
But transformed into my compass,
my barometer,
my checkpoint,
my thermometer.

Reminding me
when I have been working too hard,
when I've stayed up to late,
when I've caned it once too often
on the long weekends.

Reminding me
that this is not over…
just under control.

Because I have
a new routine,
a new habit,
and a new life.

I have new tricks,
and new hopes.

I have a new pulse,
and new fears.

I have new rhythms,
and new rhymes.

I have new freedoms,
and new deadlines.

I have both the shortest
and the longest of times.

Home

From a distance
you appear opaque,
like a jumbled
and chaotic
cityscape.

Functions, styles, vernaculars,
crawling over one another.

Competing for attention.
Hard surfaces reflecting.

The ever changing patterns
of cloud shadow
move across your face.

You intimidate.

Moving closer,
your complexities resolve.
Your eyes providing glimpses
of vibrant public space.

Gardens of quiet reflection.

The energy of Commerce.

The certainty of Law.

You draw me in...

Revealing
your diversity,

your history,
your internal logic,
your magical vistas,
your dark underbelly.

There are no maps
to finger trace your heart's
geography as I roam.

Just streets walked in discovery.
I want to call you Home.

Frostbitten

When you first
came to talk to me
I was hypnotised
by your glittering
cool transparency.
Drawn to examine
the cracks and
fissures twisting around
your opaque heart,
I touched you
and hoped that we
would never part.

Now it's over,
and sometimes
these days
it feels as though
I never even
saw you.
Back then
my touch felt
like it couldn't
even start to thaw you.

That's how it was.

Frozen against you
for all those years.

Even at your warmest,
deep inside
the folds of you,

your arse clasped tight
around my wrist,
your guts enfolded
'round my fist,

I just reached into emptiness.

A yearning never satisfied.

Afterwards,
the only thing
you ever asked
was just how deep
I'd reached inside.

A life so small
it could be measured
in inches.

Lying beside you,
numb and shuddering
with night-sweat chills,
I wondered who else had
been inside you
during the dog day afternoons
as I worked…
worried…
earned…
to pay the bills.

Some nights
alcohol thawed the ice
sufficiently to free our fists
for other uses.

More conventional
household abuses.

"Fell off my bike."
"Tripped on the stairs."
We took our turns
to make excuses…

… but only
the midnight copper
cared.

To those outside
our closeness
appeared touching.
But they
could neither see
nor feel
the tearing skin
each time I tried
to peel myself away.

Now it's over,
and I lie thawing
in the sun.
Parts of me still
black and flayed.
Parts of me still
aching
numb.

A moment smitten.

A lifetime frostbitten.

Plural Possessive

New friends in a new city.

Bathed in the afterglow of a long red night,
we talk of Burroughs and acting.
The gentle probes and brushes
of conversational archaeology
providing glimpses,
fragments of knowledge...

"Can you cook?"

We eat slivers
of exquisite rarities.
Savouring the flavour
of the recently endangered,
as the world turns
on its own spit.

Drips,
in its own spit.

And, as it thaws,
we become
soft mechanics,
picking at the entrails
to establish the connections.

Unravelling the complexities
of the New Year's couplings
when we three fucked.

Delirious.

Loved up.

Drug fucked.

Fucked up.

Loved.

As the world burned
on its own spit.

Eating his salt bread,
we talk of action
and responsibility.
Comparing our burgeoning guilt
and inadequate remedies.

"Do you recycle?"

Until, sated on his food,
we retire to the warm tension
of your (plural possessive) domesticity,
where, thinking of what's gone,
and all that I've never even held in my hand,
I feel the pain of loss,
the warmth of friendship,
the heat of desire,
the weight of your hand on my thigh.

And as he watches…
I suck on your thick tongue.
Tonguing your wet lips.

Drinking your warm spit.

Braised in the heat radiating
from his warm kitchen,
from your (plural possessive) love,
from the burning, turning,
spit roasted,
world.

It's only later,
in the sodium yellow cold
of the January night,
that the answer comes to me.

"Sure I can cook.
I just can't feed myself."

Not You

Lily white.
Rose red.
Cornflower blue.

Your face,
a conventional bouquet.

Artfully arranged.
Carefully dethorned.
Beautifully presented.

But soon
my appreciation wanes,
and, in my imagination,
petals drop,
fade,
decay.

Your scent,
brief intense intoxication,
turns to flower-water
rank stagnation.

Instead,
give me a hedgerow.
Dog-rosed,
fruit-laden and
bramble-tangled.

The layered growth of seasons,
and each season a new beginning.

Let me sit,
cat-like for hours
watching for the small movements
that will give away the secrets
that inhabit you.

Give me shelter,
as you dance in the capricious breeze.

Dapple my sunlight.

Come the night,
let me learn
your nocturnal pathways,
and if I should dive into you,
let me emerge
bloodied and juice stained.

Give me tendrils not ribbons.
Give me roots not stems.
Give me fields not vases.

Damn your bouquet.
Give me a hedgerow.

Boundaries

On our first date,
after four years
of virtual conversation,
we argued.
In part at least because
you told me that my first love,
long distance,
four thousand miles to be exact,
had been invalid.
Not love at all.
Just some romantic
adolescent thrall.

You overstepped my boundaries that night.

Our second date went rather better.
The atmosphere electric
as you granted me three wishes.
One: a bareback pub toilet fuck.
Two: a midnight trip to the local piss club.
Three: (and this the most surprising)
you accompanied me home
to sleep in bed beside me.
Something you said you'd not done in years.

Our third date,
a lazy Sunday afternoon
watching movies after a pub lunch.
No toilet fuck,
but instead
sober lovemaking
in your bed.

It was only on our fourth date,
the night before you left,
drinking midnight tea in Piccadilly,
watching tourists and the public theatre
playing out at the feet of Eros,
that I asked if you were scared of intimacy.

It's not intimacy but commitment that
scares the bejeezus out of me,
I tell you in virtual chat
a week later and two thousand two hundred twenty miles apart.

You ask if you can piss into my open heart.

Surely intimacy is the gateway
to commitment you say.

Maybe.

And maybe that's why I swing on the gate.
Enjoying the ride and the view.
Splinters in my fingers.
The sound of creaking hinges.

Never quite stepping off.
Boundaries the only things respected.

Old Wounds

Beneath the black light
of a new moon
it's been a long night
and all the old wounds
are aching.

The silence that surrounds me,
is only shattered by the hard beat
of resolutions breaking.

It's been a rough week
of strong drink
and weak wills,
and now fresh scabs
cover old scars
and I'm a new face
in all the old bars.

I'm a new ghost
in all the old haunts,
with a head full
of all the old taunts.
And when the cuts bleed
and let the dirt in,
I find my old self
under new skin,
and even daybreak
don't let the light in.

Dark Matter

Walking down Old Street,
diesel choked,
rain soaked and
colour saturated in reflected neon,
I feel the lack of stars tonight
as keenly as I feel your absence.

I step back into an alleyway
and watch the people passing by.
Heads down against the rain.

There is no wonder in the dazzle of the lights,
no company in teeming pavement crowds,
no nourishment in the fast food joints
and convenience stores that line their route.

I remember the streets of another city.
Summertime. Breathless with hot bitumen.
The silent weekend business district
offering cool canyons of refuge.

I'd press myself against the granite surfaces,
touching North in their dark, penetrating, cold,
and feeling the pleasure
first of goose bumps, then of shivers,
advancing across the bare flesh of my arms and legs
and beneath the thin fabric of summer clothes.

I want to touch the North of you.
The place my gaze never falls.
The place that never knows my curiosity,
or admiration, or concern.

The parts that I can know only obliquely.

For even if you were here,
even if the stars shone down on us tonight,
I would still be grasping at fractions.

Inferring the unknown,
like dark matter weighed in absence.

Soul Kitchen

You, me and Aretha Franklin,
ember warm
and cooking breakfast
in the Sunday kitchen
of mi casa flotante.
Rock steady
and full of soul,
we accommodate
the occasional
rock and roll,
the soft swell wake
of passing traffic.

The uncertainties
of last night's unsteadiness
forgotten in the
morning stillness,
we cook up a storm.
Swaying and
bumping hips like
backing singers,
over eggs and mushrooms
tossing on the stove.

We tear at bread
warm and fresh as the day.
The half expressed fears
and unmet needs
drunkenly kneaded
into three a.m. homecoming dough,
evaporate like our hangovers,

or the mist
rising from the water
outside the window.

And as you feed me
hot buttered toast you ask,
"What is a do-right-all-night man?"
and I remember how
you sealed my mouth
with chocolate kisses
before pulling me,
flour coated,
to the soft cocoon
of my bed.

And despite our drunken stumbling,
and the wake of passing traffic,
we accommodate the occasional
rock and roll of the boat,
as we sway our hips
from left to right,
'cos we're rock steady
in this Sunday morning soul kitchen,
for at least another night.

Metropolitan Hand-Stitched Blues

My trans-gendered
coffee shop princess
smiles rarely.
Her story etched
deep upon her face.
She looks like
a Warhol Super 8 film slide
or a lyric from Lou Reed's
"Walk On The Wild Side."

Outside,
the Sunday morning
Brick Lane punters
take a walk
on capitalism's
mild side.

Organic,
Fairtrade,
hand-stitched
and fresh-ground.

And I think that maybe
her sad kohl-eyed smile
brings me onside.
But perhaps I'm just another
Sunday morning sucker
looking for a bit
of local colour
with a cute Spanish lad
by my side.

'Cos I don't know
what scars
the make-up hides,
or the joy or the pain
that she holds inside.
And the rain falls,
and the kids cry,
and the coloured girls go.....
"Whatever"
as they walk on by.

And the only thing
that cracks
is the make up
'round her lips,
but that's not a smile.

She hands me my coffee
and keeps the change
without being asked
and I say "Goodbye,"
and walk out into the
swirling sodden colour,
wondering if I'm anything more
than the slogan on a t-shirt,
or the lyrics of a song,
or the ethical shit that I buy.

And if my new found part-time lover
is the real deal
or just a Sunday morning drive-by,
taking a walk on the wild side
with a high-risk barfly.

'Cos she aint Holly from Miami
or Candy from the island,
I aint no auteur
and he's just a Spaniard
in a cold, wet foreign town.
That kid just keeps on yelling,
and the coloured girls go "Whatever,"
and the August London rain,
just keeps on coming down.

Notme

In these tearing moments
I think of you and notme.
The train carriage rocks and rolls
like your tin tub when we make love,
and behind me,
in the hard white light,
a young black girl
sobs softly into her mobile phone;

"Please, please, please."

You said the problem is
not who I am, but who I am not.
And on reflection
in your unflinching mirror
I know this to be the truth.
For the things that I am not
are not the me I am with you.

But which is true for me my love,
and which my love is true for you?
Which of us do you see?
Is it me, or notme?

I gaze at the train window
and wonder who it is
staring back at me
in its double edged reflection.
Caught in the unflinching glare
of the carriage lights,
as behind me
the young girl rocks softly,
and outside

London glows and fumes my love.
And I must cross its cold and dirty heart tonight
if I'm to be with you my love.

And is this safe or not safe,
this journey we've embarked upon?

The city streets are stripped of
their morning suited sheen
by the hard truth of a winter's night.
The tyres of my bike will find
each crack and imperfection,
like your hands on my
bare flesh in the thin tin shelter
of our bow-stowed beds.

And when at last I reach you love,
and I look into your eyes,
who will be reflected there my love?

In these breathless moments
I think of you and notme.
The train carriage
groans and rasps
like my cold steel hull
on wet stone walls.
And behind me,
in the hard white light
a young black girl
sobs softly into her mobile phone;

"Please, please, please,
this is such a long journey."

Pocket Garden

Walking home at midnight.
The scent of gardens
tumbles over iron railings,
and at each rosebush
I stop and pluck
a single blossom,
stowing it safely
against my chest
as I replay the night's events
from ten different angles.

Carrying the aromas
of Liverpool Road
home in my breast pocket,
as my mouth carries
the lingering memory
of your tobacco flavoured tongue,
and the ambiguities
of our goodnight kiss.

The next morning
my shirt lies crumpled
on the bedroom floor,
smelling of beer
and cigarette smoke,
and the petals of our pocket garden
are scattered at the foot of the bed
already fading
like my fragmented memories.

I pull back the curtains
and face the day with certainty.

No More Words

I've tried to walk a mile in your shoes,
but my feet bled,
and the backs broke,
and you shouted at me
as you walked a mile
barefoot to collect them back.

I've tried to play the games that you lose,
but the dice rolled my way,
and I cleared the table
leaving you with a
bad debt still to pay,
and nothing left to play for.

I've tried to heal the places you bruise,
but my touch hurt
and the medication made it worse,
and the flowers died,
so I left the room
as you called the nurse.

I've tried to make the choices you choose,
so I've smashed the mirrors
and pulled the blinds down,
and I've torn all of the lines out,
and there's no more
words to write now.

Meniscus

Breaking through
the surface tension,
I am born again.

Baptismal rivulets
form on far from
perfect skin.

Cured of boils,
sores and all
inflammatory stigmata.
But not without the scars
of their removal
that I shall carry with me
to the grave.

This holy water
does not wash me clean.

Surfacing I brush away
the clinging web of
past encounters,
tears and laughter.

But from the skein
pick out the threads
that I shall keep
to weave the mesh
that will enfold these bones
in the hereafter,
when once again,
and finally,
betrayed by flesh.

A shroud of all that went before.

And when at last I lie
in all my past enfolded,
free of flesh and cured of scars,
my brittle bones bleached clean,

I shall unpick
this fabric I have woven,
in quiet eternal reverie.

Kandinsky's Tuba

In the cooling
early dusk of May,
the sunset pyrotechnics
have all but burned away.

Across the blue and pink
pearlescent sky,
swallows dip
weave and dive.

The dying day finely balanced
on the cusp of spring and summer.

Horse chestnut flowers,
waxy candles,
light the evening,
as geese protect their goslings
from the squabbling of scribbled coot chicks.

The hiss of birds and bull rush breezes
punctuated by the silent grace of the heron,
teaching patience.

Lush abundance breathes in heaving swirls
like Vincent's wheat fields.

And in this moment,
the essence of all that is
and all that will be
rushes through me,
and my soul vibrates
to the sound of
Kandinsky's wild tuba.

Tomorrow

I want to believe in tomorrow.

I want to able to say,
"I'll see you 'round then…"
and mean it.

But some days this town
just feels too dissolute
too big,
too fast,
too irresolute,
for anything to really last.

It feels as though
even if I go and dance
for five minutes,
leaving you at the bar,
I'll return to find you gone.
The whole crowd moved on
in the time it takes
to change a record.

But how are we ever
supposed to find our song
or write our story?
When even whilst you're talking to me
you're looking over my shoulder.

It's all death or glory.

But I want a love that develops
like a slow patina over time.

Accreting meaning with each meeting.

A gradual blurring of the lines
between yours…
ours…
mine…

I don't want to have to offer
three time slots in the next fortnight,
or be fitted in
between a movie and a dinner date,
only to be squeezed out
because you're running late

(again).

I don't want to have to say "yes"
when I mean "no"
because saying "no" this time
might mean there won't be a next time
until sometime next year,
when we bump into each other
by chance once more and start over.
Because in all that time
we've not met anyone else
that we really connect with.

Just a series of hurried fumbles
and first dates.
An endless gentleman's "excuse me"
of getting-to-know-yous
and getting-to-know-mes.
A looped tape of over-rehearsed life stories.

But this time it seems as though
maybe there's a new story,
still unwritten,
hidden between the same old lines.

Like there's something in your eyes
I could believe in.

Like I want to believe in tomorrow.

Like I want to be able to say,
"I'll see you 'round then…"
and mean it.

WHAT THE HEART NEEDS TO HEAL

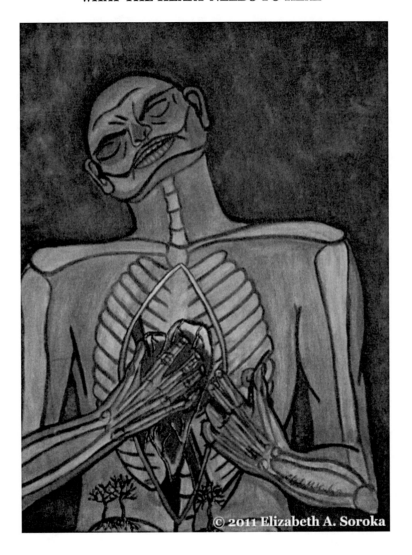

Memories Of A Balloon Festival

Legs still heavy with sleep
we climb the hill
in the early half light,
laden with blankets and hampers
to witness the annual spectacle
of the dawn lift.

A field of hot-air balloons sway tethered.

This morning we are told
they may be unable to rise over the sleeping city
for fear of winds too high above the ground
to be felt by those of us gathered to watch.

Anticipation punctured
but our spirits lifted
by the excitement of the pre-dawn preparations
still underway amidst drifts
of barbeque smoke and champagne bubbles.

We strike up conversation with our neighbours,
newlyweds radiating happiness,
who share our gentle adventure
and over-catered breakfast.

The sun rises
and the warming air
breaks the overnight stillness
summoning down the spoiling breeze
rippling and cracking
the deflating fabric
of the balloons.

Feeling the early morning magic
beginning to unweave
we gather our small party
and make to leave.

In that moment of packing
something strikes her
and with missionary purpose
she returns to the newlyweds
to pass on her view,
that love finds the one
who will teach the hard lessons
that the heart needs to feel
if the heart is to heal.

Perhaps they'll think her mad
but you and I understand her hope
that as their days together lengthen
and turbulence begins to disturb
their early dawn magic
they will recall these words
if not who said them or where.

By her action she becomes
fairy godmother
guardian angel
crone.

But even she does not feel
the squeeze of your hand,
and may never know
the words that she speaks
echo true even closer to home.

Dredged

The action it seems
has happened elsewhere.

The rain falling on distant
unvisited hills.

Here in the lowlands
I wake to a landscape
transformed by floodwaters
which have risen silently
and unnoticed in the darkness.

Beneath the impassive surface
powerful currents lift the silt of years.
Flotsam swirls in lazy gyres
and long-dry channels
are swept clear of detritus.

Beyond the far horizon
the unseen storm moves on.
Flood waters recede
leaving only jetsam
and new pools of quiet reflection.

Tears in a landscape.

Sunlight will dry the tear pools.
Scavengers will pick over
the strand-line debris for fuel and shelter
and the fresh-cut channels
will one day run clear,
when, in some other season,
the rain eventually falls here.

A Warning

There are vampires my love.
They move amongst us
like the walking dead.

And those like you
who take a joy in life
whose very presence lights up a room
who blaze a trail across both night and day
who flare and spark like comet tails
with energy to spare,
it is such as you who should beware
for it is such as you who are their prey.

Please, my love, don't be misled.
They are not like the characters
in films or songs or books.
They don't have Boris Karloff looks
or Michael Jackson's killer hooks.
They don't require a full lit moon
to lead you like a lamb to slaughter.
In fact they look like me and you,
like anybody's sons or daughters.

They may even thrill you too.

But hold them close and you will feel
it's by the lack of inner fire
that burns within the living heart
that they may be distinguished.
Perhaps they never felt the spark of visceral combustion
or perhaps, for some infernal reason,
the internal flame has been extinguished.

And there are many myths my love.
They will not live a life eternal.
They inhabit light as well as dark.
You may gaze at their reflection
in the restaurant table glass
and garlic dough-ball starters
will offer no protection.

It's not your blood they're after either.

It's the mesmerizing way
your eyes bring sparkle to the gloom,
your easy untamed laughter
that attracts them.

They believe the flame that
burns so bright within your heart
may be captured like a firefly in a jar,
tamed and made to serve them too.

But they are husks, the walking dead,
whose fires cannot be reignited.
Their need and jealousy are not
the loving deeds required to feed
the flames of fires such as yours.

So be warned my love.

For hard though it may be to believe it
your flame will dim and gutter out,
that burning light behind your eyes expire.

That sacred fire will die.

But you will carry on in their damned company
and together you will trawl these halls
seeking out the flames of strangers
who still illuminate the gathering dark.

So when I see
your spark
your fire
your flaming eyes
your burning heart
I want you to know
that there are vampires.

They are near and far
and they are here and there.

They are everywhere.
So please, my love, beware.

Eclipsed

I miss your familiar greeting kiss,
the one that's moved to cheek from lips,
your direct gaze whose eyes now slide away
your heart once open now eclipsed.

I wonder if, with patience, I should wait
or like some hardy Argonaut
should try to circumnavigate
this obstacle that lies between us.

Are you are the guardian of the fleece
that could redeem us?

Or just some decoy,
some distraction placed along the way.
A siren call for this unwary sailor
who maybe should not linger here,
but instead should simply sail away
and try his luck on other shores
perhaps more welcoming than yours.

But still I miss that greeting kiss
and so each time we meet
I keep my arms down by my sides,
tied to the imaginary mast
that I should not reach out and grasp
or hold too long
and give away the fact
that in my ears
I can still hear your siren song.

Becalmed, bewildered and confused,
I hope the shadow may yet move away.

In the meantime I recall the golden
light that shines behind it
and wonder if not me then who will be
the lucky traveller that finds it.

Rushes

Sunlight
twice reflected
ripples across my ceiling
as I lie on that same couch
remembering sun-warmed skin,
gooseflesh and the cool
of your caress.

The afternoon that I
punctured your disinterest
plays out like a home movie in my head,
soundless and complete with
handheld picture shake.

The bright sunlight bleaches out the images
projected onto the blank screen of my memory,
rendering them colourless and void of detail.

We never did pull down the blinds that afternoon.
Passers-by glimpsed flashes of our nakedness
on their Saturday afternoon promenade.

At the time it didn't seem to matter.

Now I realise
that we were always
overexposed.

Let's Dance

We're all dying.
Every last one of us.
You. Me. He. She.
We're all fucking dying.

Some of us bear the cross
of knowing the approximate date
of our demise or its likely cause.
Our continued health
a confection of pills and powders.
A scaffold of medication
that may give out at any time
causing this apparently robust facade
to crumble into dust.

We may choose
to use this knowledge
in a multitude of ways.
We may create a filigree
of such delicate knowing beauty
that it moves those who view it
to join us in our mourning tears.

Or we may take it hard
and crassly force
the cold clods of despair
into a rough and lumpen mass
that we smash into the faces
of those who pass us by,
just so that we may watch in fascination
as they bleed with us and cry.

Even those oblivious
to the slowly unwinding mechanism
of the timing device
may fall victim
to the ruptured valve
of a dickey ticker.
We are *all* dying.

So let's dance!

Let's turn this funeral dirge into a reel.
Let's a build a fire and spin around
the pyre of all the lives that could have been.

The suicide. The still born son.
The "gone too soon."
The victim of the hit and run.
Come take this girl and hold her close.
Dance with her, and as you waltz,
feel the rapidly dividing cells
the galloping metastases.
Caress the dark and troubling growth
the scars of the mastectomy.

Throw a party for the dispossessed
the diseased and the emotionally distressed.
Everyone's invited even those who haven't got it yet.

So let's build the fire
and stoke the flames.

Let's dance our fucking lives away.
We're all just dying anyway.

Geezer

"Geezer!"
"Matey!"
Back slaps and head rubs.
Sweaty hugs and play punches.

His arm slips around my shoulder
as we chat like long lost brothers
about nothing in particular.

In fact we've never met before.
It's the instant friendship of the dance floor.
The camaraderie of tattoos and haircuts
shared drinks and loved up back rubs.

And this geezer's gorgeous.
Straight of course.
Thick set and rugged with dancing eyes
(the drugs perhaps but never mind)
a body builder's arms and thighs.

We chat a while then say goodbye.
As we part I catch his eye
and tell him that it's not a come-on
but I like to tell a man he's handsome.

For a moment I feel the fear
that stretches back across the years
of prejudice and pain and hate.

I wonder if he'll punch me out
but he just turns and grins and shouts,

"Not bad yourself mate"
and disappears into the crowd.

In my heart I feel a swelling pride
(the drugs again perhaps but never mind)
not in myself or even in my new found brother
but in the nameless, faceless others
who faced down ignorance and fear
across the unforgiving years.

The camp queens
the has-beens
the girls in drag.
The old gay men
who never had
the chance to feel
another's love.
Just a furtive fumble
a push,
a shove,
a smack across the face,
a kick,
"You fuckin' queer."
"You filthy prick."

The ones who couldn't pass for straight.
The ones who'd been the bashers bait
since they were ten, or nine, or eight.

The ones who let the bruises heal
who re-emerged as strong as steel.
Clad in sequins, armed with wit
a clutch-bag sized survival kit
of lippy, blusher and twenty Bensons,
a miniature of "mother's medicine."

The ones who built a scene together.
A clan that holds you like a lover.
A bitchy roller coaster ride
that can spit you out the other side.
A glorious sparkling seedy creature,
that's withstood the insults piled upon her.
Lost some to madness, drink, virus,
and many more to fear and violence.

So now I stand amongst my peers.
Gays, straights and in-betweeners.
A time and place where I can be
whatever I may I choose to be.

So as the geezer disappears
I feel the ghosts of all those faggots
those marys and those queers,
a roll-call down the unforgiving years,
and give thanks to
those who brought me here.

Testament

I wear
your bruises
like tattoos.

Admiring
the blue and purple marbled
patterns spreading out across my skin.

Silent witness to your weakness.

Visible testament to my strength.

The bleeding cuts
the closest I will ever get
to letting you
inside me.

Two Strong Hands

1.

You need two strong hands for a good game.

First time it seemed fate dealt us both promise
but your fear trumped my hope
and we both retired hurt.

By the time of our chance reunion
you'd traded fear for reason
and over coffee we shared details
of distant not-yet loves.
Tracing the trajectories of passed on promises.

As shy eyes met and smiles flickered
we mapped out six degrees of separation.
Me to him.   Him to me.   Me to you.
You to him.   Him to you.   You to me.

Two victims of geography and bad timing
seeking comfort in each other's bravery
and half expressed commitments.

2.

As weak spring sunshine warmed to summer
coffee-shop smiles sweetened to intimacy.

Two strong hands found each other
in the back row of a darkened theatre
and entwined like the bodies on stage.

Together they choreographed a new dance.

Prelude to the drama yet to unfold.
Picking out the fine details,
of soft arm hair, hard stubble,
warm breath, moist lips.

Fingers dancing new promises
in the early summer heat.

Later we cycled through night time streets
and at each junction you shared sugar from your pocket
or leaned across and kissed my neck
before the lights changed
and you disappeared into the traffic's weave.

In a basement club we danced with abandon.
Heads back and laughing.
Losing ourselves in dance floor kisses.
Creating breathless pirouettes
illuminated by the stage lights of a city night.

3.

The next day you phone
to tell me your heart is sad.
It was too perfect.
You miss him.
You.   Miss.   Him.

I *know* that I made a perfect night.
I moved you to tears when we made love.
I ate strawberries from your mouth.
I wore you like a leather glove.

But we are victims of geography and bad timing.
I cannot be him for you.

You cannot be him for me.

And then I wonder,
what if we only have
so many perfect nights in us?
And what if I used up all my aces
on dances and promises
and strawberry kisses?

What if,
when the time comes
and the night demands perfection,
all I have left is deuces?

What then?

4.

Summer turns to autumn
as the coffee turns bitter
in my unkissed mouth,
and you pack
and make your preparations
to fly south for the winter.

And still we dance.
Just further apart.

This time when the night falls
with a hand unheld
and an aching heart
I cry tears of loneliness.

Tears I've never cried
in all these years of solitude.

For who on earth can spare them?

But tonight I let them flow
in the hope that our geography
may be altered irrevocably by them.

Because you know we'd wear our hearts on sleeves
but we've lost the shirts on which to bear them.
So it's spades and clubs tattooed on skin
that's worn to worthless paper thin,
suits of diamonds glittering on moonlit cheeks
and breath that reeks of whiskey and gin.

What if we're dealing cards from a single deck?

One game. One hand. One chance. That's it.

Because it seems like I'm playing with a pack
with no hearts and no jacks
so it's no wonder that I keep on losing.

You need two strong hands for a good game.

And you've cashed yours in tonight.

Leaving me at the table
with an unheld hand,
memories of strawberry kisses,
weaving tail lights,
dancing fingers,
a face full of diamonds
and one less perfect night.

How Men Are

She knows how men are.
Of course she does.
She's raised two.

So perhaps it's no surprise
when her youngest son
sits her down and says
"There's something I need to tell you, Mum"
that tears well in her weary eyes.

Of course he doesn't understand.

In the months that follow,
of coming to terms,
though never to blows,
there are many words
that would have been better left unsaid.

All manner of fears
horrors and dreads
because of what he may
or may not do in bed
or out of it, and with whom.

Amongst the dire prophesies
of heartbreak, doomed love, and disease
(too many of which have turned out true it seems)
one in particular stood out for him.
"It's different with girls" she said.
She should know. She's raised one.
"With them you're always scared
because you know one day they'll have to deal with men..."

She didn't need to elaborate.

They could both
fill in the silence
with visions
of distance and drink
infidelity and violence.

"I never thought
I'd have to worry
about that again"
she sighs.

You see she knows how men are.

But as the years roll by
he learns to navigate this world he's chosen
and finds new words
that could have filled that silence.

He finds nurturing and strength,
love and comradeship
and self reliance.
He finds tenderness and tears,
self doubt and barely hidden fears.

He finds but cannot quite describe
the mystery that hides within the heart of masculinity.

He wonders if she found it too
and if she shared it with her only daughter.
Because surely she knows how men are?
Of course she does.

She married one, didn't she.

Ghosts

In the late December night
backlit by bus shelter advertisements
I watch your moving lips.

Each exclamation
forms a small cloud
in the cold dense air.

Wraiths of meaning
hanging in the spaces
that separate us.

I wonder how long
your words will haunt me
after they have died on your lips,
and whether I will
keep their memory alive
by weaving them into
late-night fireside stories
that raise hairs
on the necks of those
gathered to listen.

As the night bus approaches
and we say goodbye
I watch your word ghosts
dissolve into the darkness
and I wonder if I ever believed in them.

We Are Monuments

We have a history.
A history of villains and heroes,
of battles fought and lost
and of battles won.

As histories go
it is largely unmarked by monuments
to great lives or hard won victories.

There are no cemeteries
honouring the fallen,
though they are legion.

Ours is a history
both stronger than stone
and as ephemeral as life itself.

It is not the history written in headlines.
It is a history of lives lived in love.

For we are not the blood of lone victims spilled on pavements.
We are the pooled candle wax of the one hundred gathered in vigil.

We are not hatred, or intolerance, or oppression
We are the voices raised in protest.

We are reasoned argument.
We are equality written into law.

We are not illness, ignorance or disease.
We are carers, educators and healers.

And so it is that we fight our battles;
with reason
with compassion
with learning
with friendship.

And with love we stitch together
the ragged quilt of our community.
Rag tag ends of ill matched colour,
crafted by the hands of millions.
Handed down from generation to generation.

And with love we build our institutions.

Not nuclear, high walled and exclusive,
but incandescent, welcoming beacons of liberty.
Openhearted, generous, accepting.

For we have a history.
It is still being written.
And we are its monuments.

Jesus and Me

This Christmas
I'm communicating
with Jesus directly.

By email.

No obfuscating intermediary.
No pulpit sermons.
No letters to Santa.
No papal bullshit.

Me and Jesus have got something personal going.

It was early one Saturday morning
start of December
when he entered my life.

It was Advent
and I was a little drunk
when he appeared miraculously at my side.
After some preliminaries
of the most ecumenical kind
he slipped me half an E
and we celebrated
our unholy communion.

It wasn't long until I was on my knees
singing hallelujahs.
Marvelling at the miracle
of transubstantiation
as our communal disco biscuit
turned flesh in my mouth
and I swallowed him whole.

We didn't swap numbers
but, whilst I may have doubted
his intentions,
he has appeared to me
no less than three times
since that fateful night.

The grotto of each visitation
the dubious location
of the Joiner's Arms.
That grotty, overcrowded celebration
of the carpenter's
rough-hewn charms.

Each time I have awoken
the next morning
a little hungover
a little sore
blissfully sure in the knowledge
that I have had Jesus in me.

But it's Christmas,
so he has returned to his family.
In Madrid.
For the holidays.

And we are communicating by email.

From: Jesus A. Garcia
Subject: Hey Sexy

Because I have a friend in Jesus.

That be the lesson.
Now let us pray.

I Don't Want Much

I don't want much.

I just want to bury my head
in the pits of your arms
and to sniff you like glue.

I want to smell
the scent of the sweat
of my arse on your beard.

I want to remember
what your tongue felt like
licking me there.

I want to taste
myself on your lips.

I want to wear bruises
inflicted by the thrust
of your hips.

I want to be quenched
by the taste of your piss
when I'm gasping with thirst.

And if we should sleep
I want to wake first
so I can lie here
counting my blessings,
counting your charms,
counting the delicate hairs on your arms.

When you wake up
I want you to miss me
whilst I go to the kitchen
to make coffee for you.

I want to make history.

I want to take on the world
in a bare knuckle fight
feeling no fear
because you're there at my back
in a rearguard defence
against every attack.

In a lull in the battle
I'll lean my head back and laugh
and suck the blood
from your lips.

I'll bind up your fists
where the knuckles are flayed.

I want to be sure that I won't be betrayed.

I guess it might seem
like I'm looking for love
but to be brutally honest,
if push comes to shove
I don't want that much.

Right now I'd make do with a text,
or the sound of your voice on the phone.
I'd be happy to know
that I'm not alone
and that you want me too.

Because I feel like
a recidivist addict
who's enjoying the habit,
and I just want to bury my face
in the pits of your arms
and to sniff you like glue.

D.I.L.F.

Excuse me madam
Is that your husband?
Or perhaps just
the father of your child?
That guy with the pushchair
in the grocery aisle…

Because the three day stubble
and the rough-neck fashion
would make me look twice
on any occasion,
but it's the child in his care
that's making me stare.
He's a daddy I'd like to fuck.

And I know that
it doesn't make any sense.
Biologically speaking
it makes no difference to me
if he's fertile or firing blanks.
Besides I'd settle for a blow job
or a mutual wank.

But there's something so virile
about a man with a child
that even a middle aged bloke
with very few charms
is quickly transformed
by a child in arms
into a daddy I'd like to fuck.

Tell me who's that older guy?

The one with the smile lines
around his eyes
when he gives you
that protective look.

Did he nurture you
in the crook of his arm
and spend years of his life
keeping you safe from harm?
His careworn face
and his greying locks
give him the distinguished look
of a silver fox
and despite his age
with his rugby build
he looks like he'd still
be good for a ruck.

I know he's your Dad
and it's really not polite
but I'd love to borrow him
for the night.
He's a daddy I'd like to fuck.

So when you notice me smiling
at your family group
it's not that I'm being sentimental,
it's something much more elemental.

But please don't drag him off
down the vegetable aisle
when you notice the hungry look in my eyes.

You see I don't mean to be disrespectful
and I'm not about to make a move,

besides I'm sure if I did that he wouldn't approve,
but that bloke on your arm
has set something stirring
and the fact he's a dad
just makes him much more alluring.

So why not be proud
or little bit smug?

Even tip me a wink.

Because I'm hardly a threat.

I'm just a gay bloke out shopping
who's down on his luck
and he's a daddy I'd like to fuck.

Two Thousand And Seven

It was an odd year.

It was always the odd years
when you'd fly in
bringing something unexpressed.

Unconditional.

The exuberant firework immediacy of a whip, cracked.

Lines of desire stretched across oceans.

A shared story woven into music.
A tapestry of handwritten liner notes
unpacked, folded, sorted and stowed
amongst the meagre possessions
retained from the firestorm of my recent past.

Pressed beneath the weight of distant memories.

Meanings teased from between
the warp and weft of a misplaced decade
threaded across the spaces between our chosen paths.

So many ways
to say the things
we leave unsaid.

To mark the passing of time.

To share our gains and losses.

Two redeemed sinners
bearing crosses.

But never our hearts.

Until that night
when you lifted your shirt
to show me the inked memorial
of yours.

A sinewed shrine illuminated
by the shining light of a votive candle
bearing one name.

Mine.

Adrift in the sparse cocoon
of my new life
I lifted my shirt in return
and showed you that same light.

Reflected.

Glinting on the polished armour
of my iron lung.

The machinery
that kept me breathing evenly
through each of those
ten years.

The dependency
that I called freedom.

Caught in a moment of truth
we lowered our shirts.

Chose flight.

Returned to the even paths
of our separate lives.

And waited for an odd year.

Sunflower Promises

The first winds of autumn
tug at too thin summer dresses.

Forcing sunflowers
into their final bows.
Heads heavy with promises.

One by one
I let go of my misgivings
like so many wind-burnt leaves.
Surrendering myself to the season
and the possibility of renewal.

Meanwhile
your patient gardener
brings sunshine.

Weakened by the journey north.

Strong enough
to keep the frost
from thwarting
the soft new shoots,
emerging tentative and unseen
from these scarred
and blackened roots.

Like the sunflowers
we bow our heads
to the elements
unsure if our promises
will survive the coming winter.

With the patience
of gardeners,
and of forests,
with the persistence of water
and the constancy of rocks,
we hope for bounty
and await the coming spring.

The One Who

Over coffee she asks
"Is he The One?"

I blush and look away,
shrug and mutter
something non-committal.

Because I don't know
if he's The One.
Or even what that really means.
Or whether I believe
in these binary distinctions.

But there are some things that I do know.

I know he is the one
for whom my heart
has skipped more beats
than his quick feet
on thirteen years of dirty dance floors.

I know he is the one
whose gaze, whose touch
I've never flinched from.
Whether those dark brown eyes
have flashed
with anger, fear
or adoration.

I know he is the one
who lives his life in grooves,
and sometimes wears them into ruts.

I know at times he shrinks so small
it seems he's hardly there at all.

I also know that sometimes
when he walks he struts.

I know he is the one who fills
the empty spaces of my heart with joy,
just like he fills a room with laughter.

I know he's always been my Handsome Man
and that I've always been his Boy.

And then she breaks the pause
that all these thoughts inhabit
and asks me simply
if I love him.

This time I look
and meet her eye
and tell her that
I'm not sure what love is,
or if I know for certain how to give it,
but that he's the one
who makes me want to try.

Because until now
life's just been a theory,
and he's the one
who makes me want to live it.

about Mark Walton

Mark Walton inhabits the back waters and the in-between places. He writes in order to share the realities of the life he lives, feels, dreams and observes. In doing so he seeks to shine a light into the darker recesses, to celebrate the magic of the ordinary and to bring the marginal and the oblique into plain view.

He lives and performs in London, England.

also from Epic Rites Press

A Bellyful Of Anarchy by Rob Plath
Hellbound by David McLean
The Broken And The Damned by Jason Hardung
Doing Cartwheels On Doomsday Afternoon by John Yamrus
Dead Reckoning by Todd Moore
Crudely Mistaken For Life by Wolfgang Carstens
Laughing At Funerals by David McLean
The Epic Rites Journal: Building A Better Bomb
There's A Fist Dunked In Blood Beating In My Chest by Rob Plath
Blood And Greasepaint by Karl Koweski
Can't Stop Now! by John Yamrus
Crunked by Jack Henry
We're No Butchers by Rob Plath
An Age Of Monsters by William Taylor Jr.

www.epicrites.org